Wabi-Sabi

(Till the last moon I lived)

RASHMEEN KAPOOR

Published by InkQuills Publishing House
www.inkquills.in

First Edition 2023
All Rights Reserved. Copyright © 2023
ISBN: 978-93-90567-45-4

The views and opinions expressed in this book are the author's own and the facts are as reported by them, and the publisher is not in any way liable for the same.

This book has been published in good faith that the work of the author is original. All efforts have been taken to make the material error-free. However, the publisher disclaims the responsibility.

This is a work of fiction. Names, Characters, Places and incidents are product of author's imagination. Any resemblance to any actual persons, living or dead, events or locales is entirely coincidental. No part of this publication may be reproduced, transmitted, or stored in a retrieval system, in any form or by any means, electronic, mechanical, photocopying, recording or otherwise, without the prior permission of the publisher.

This book is dedicated to the spiritual power following me, protecting me, guiding me, and loving me throughout my life with also the experiences we all come across in our unconscious means! We learn and grow, that's life!

ACKNOWLEDGEMENTS

Words and a page would be less when it comes to thanking and acknowledging people who played their role in making this dream possible. Still, let me try.

Above all, let me, first thank the spiritual power that has been guiding me, and loving me throughout my life. Nothing is above that. Whatever I can do is because of the strength I got from almighty to pursue it.

After that, I would like to mention my father Late Sri Surinder Singh Kapoor. I'm very sure that no father in the world could ever love his daughter, the way my father always did. His love is beyond this mortal world. Whatever I can do involves a great part of his love and blessings.

Coming next, my mother, my maternal Uncle, and my younger brother for supporting and loving me unconditionally. The faith and trust that my family has in me are beyond one's imagination.

I'm able to put this book into your hand with their love and support as well.

It will be an injustice if I do not mention my friend Kavya Sahgal for being my best motivator and supporter since the day I have started writing professionally.

Last, but not least, let me thank Abhisar Garg, founder of InkQuills Publishing House for having trust in my work. He has always been a dear friend more than just a publisher for me.

Contents

1

Table 20

What sort of eyes are these? Coaxing me to attend the same
Mango punch biscuits with aroma of fresh roasted coffee
served at the initial mornings near church gate street, lane 2;

A glee to notice grey hair,
wearing Charlie's fragrance was worth creating
an Inferno that doesn't made me feel ashamed to re-think
about my age of wearing colourful stockings
with dotted Rapunzel hairband;

Crossing my fingers again for some "hocus pocus"
to happen Between a 'Twenties' and grey-haired table no.20,
by breaking away every edge of boundary,
I really want to reach you;

Single or Taken? divorced or unhappy?
Professor or artist?
Will my strokes of liner able to attract him or
he would just be grossed in reading "The Independent";

And the list of questions engaging me,
with the disengagement of ruthless and

hopeless years on the benches of Scotland
Alone with my hot chocolate mug,

Should I verbalize my thoughts?
but what if it spoils weeks of wearing a searing silence,
his plum pastries and my graded infatuation have already
taken me away to add 'new contact in my phone list ';

Eight Sunday's now!
my glares still eat those gentle and reliable tongue,
And like a little candy girl waiting to nod for our first date,
still not overcome what sort of eyes are these?

2

With love to Belfast

Maybe a flinch that is bothered
Since the day your visa arrived,
Our music has troubled me
For the first time in packing your suitcase
With books and frequent sobs;

Can I pack my fathoms of cuddles too?
Maybe you need that under a tree
After your long lecture ends.
Don't trust foreign air,
they will make you sick.

Leaving my greatest romance for two years
On lands of Ireland
Stable on this longing table,
hope you miss my golden hair
And laughing lips!

I don't want our love to be as heavy as carriages that is swept out in wonder parks one day
because of the distance it has of thousand miles,
But ours is like ballads of the poem
that I wrote for you after several

Dreamy meets that reached you

through rains.

I wish you to miss me,

But not too much miss me either!

Will knock your dreams during

Saturday dawn's

Wearing peach and your given Pandoras,

Every weekend staircases

Of St. Anne's cathedral will wait for you

to explore till the last window

Of museums,

Don't worry!

Will shook my head

For every long talks and walks;

I promise I won't quarrel again, but please pack my tight cuddles again.

I know you need smiles to receive you there,

Just close your eyes

I will meet you there.

My love is never like a Persian carpet

that seems beautiful but unreal,
Neither it is like Northern lights
that fulfil souls for seconds,
But it will be that uninterrupted good music,
that will hold you during Blake midnight.

Wait!
I have extra luggage of loyalties that has bonded us for years,
I know our adultery won't knock at blind doors.

Realize my existence with the
aromas of Palmolive candles
When you plan to tune guitars,
I will light them too with vanilla scoops;

Our music may trouble you sometimes,
But remember the glass of whiskey
And pack of cigars
Will never be a last resort,
And you know it's too risky.

I certainly don't want to be your

trampled flower,
After the goodbyes at the airport,
But that sandwich of passion
And sensation that is making you
work hard there.

Wish to place you at that pedestal
When people see
And worship a man who is mine,
And that relation
Which is like an irrevocable vow.

Will wait on Saturday, dawn's
With bundle of purple Poppies.
Till then, you bring the warmth of your winter rooms,
And here I will hold summers welcoming you.

I genuinely believe love makes people good,
Packing good luck and a pinch of romance
to make you bloom;

I know there is a listener called God in heaven

Who will help to communicate my longing

and joy because I know our

Never ending telepathy works

Like never before.

3

Under the sky

Under a banyan tree, the night I asked him to sit beside me,

let's discuss stories of sky and stars tonight

since intimacy doesn't mean parting ways after the last moon;

Will talk about everything like twinkles, mountains, morning
sleepy Dawn's, foliage without lurking each other's taste;

Was that just a casual ecstasy?

I asked in a stuttered tone; he said casual or not so casual
those tiny droplets of mindless excitement will vanish away
one day;

Shunned for a long, but he is benevolent I know,

and tried just to remove the known veil like 'veil of
separation';

Let me gasp you gulp you with my eyes for last, want to taste
drizzles from my collarbones, let me live in orchards of
reveries till dawn as it gives illusionary peace;

wait, let me sit for a while, exhibiting things alone

let me release that we won't cherry pluck further,

whole pizzas will be eaten by alone,

a cappuccino will not be served with hopes further,

but let me say I will leave us with the heart that aches from
loving, and feeling and caring in every way possible,
I am proud in a way I poured love in everything I did.
For me, that's 'liberation' means

Will make merry for the last time,
I know we cannot see celestials together again,
jolting thoughts with eager eyes
Will you be all my metaphors tonight?

4

Flares of my love

Falling for one, creates thousands of galaxies inside me.
where you just can't let them go;
At one place it gives a bubble of solemn peace
but it soon lapses with a fear to lose in a blink;
Who are you to me, don't know,
but yeah, whoever you are I see
a glimpse of Estonian wilderness,
till the time, heart says yes,
till the time my eyes seek tik-tik waiting,
till the time my skin breaths that I am loved,
till the time I have my breath that is not anxious at 2;
till the time I seek worthy sunrise with you,
flared with pious colours of love without
loving any less than the other.

I would never wish my love to be like a bride's henna'
and like its color, but mine will be like that
secret sacrifice that will be unknown ever
that's my only prayer and playing card.
Because I know I love and love and love and love.

Will not serve my body wrapped with a Hippocratic mind,
but mine will be quietly praying for you.
Will not fight for which god to pray
to because for me faithful eyes will
only be my home and hope;

I just long for those fingers running on my head to
give me peaceful sleep till my grave yells for more peace.
longing for that tight cuddle after one loses to
stand again.
And I promise I will be that 'angel '
Because I will be just light, where you look and smile.
I wish to be your that smile,
that your body cannot control as joy

5

Am I still alive?

That dark unfaithful sky gazing while I was sitting on
that broken bench, like that of my fragmented soul;

Couldn't generalize that day's weather,
why it was so solemn and heavy, in spite of birds chirping,
may be clouds turned blunt with my moon;

That emptiness was eating me inside like mere scavenger,
taking the very strand of my inner sober peace,
strange distress was the only dwell I could hire for,
since my eyes knows my struggle better

With my brain-dead, body numb,
but bizarre heart still knows how to beat,
may be because nostalgia of guitars still plays in my background unconsciously;

Never knew this desolation would randomly
ask for my own sacrifice, and this filth in some meets would be
a disappointment
yeah, I craved for people to share their piece

of happiness that includes 'relics n relish ',
but they turned out to be mere mocks of dishonesty;

The most wonderful part is when they left like a mere creep,
so that one day I fetch my own 6 feet
grave with this feeling of emptiness;

Like Dawn dead winters, and lifeless 'gulmohars' that
are stuck with freeze life like me
swollen nasal after for years;

Will inform all my rupture to guardian angels,
of how every life was taken away by life itself.
Till then, let me lament the loss of my peace
and give tribute to all my struggles bravely.

6

Subtle Morning

Yes, I am not a Hebrew person consolidated with ancient cradle,

have learned to absorb the rhythm of experiences that people yell;

I love the splashes of sun hitting my bosom,

where my eyelashes are still not ready to move;

Where pages by John Donne are still rolling on

my table,

asking me to smell that hot coffee served in archaic metal;

My feline family under my bed are my best guards,

protecting me from rotten faithless erotic dreams;

Putting on my straps again with the compliment

of strawberry gloss,

preparing my forehead to sense outside

crowd who remains a fallacy in this life.

I will knock on my shelf tonight

Speculating Darwin's fittest again

Don't worry! I will be tactful

this time till I finish reading till edge,

Promising my seventh shelf to not weep, to see my sky in the moonlight.

The existence carries a dilemma of 'why me every time' kind of hours,

I know the burden is dull-witted but has a reality though.

Manifesting to love, or to be loved, but the dilemma is for whom?

I need to stop flaring my inks at my thinnest pieces, thinking that it makes the midnight better,

But it's the same!!

7

To the soul I miss

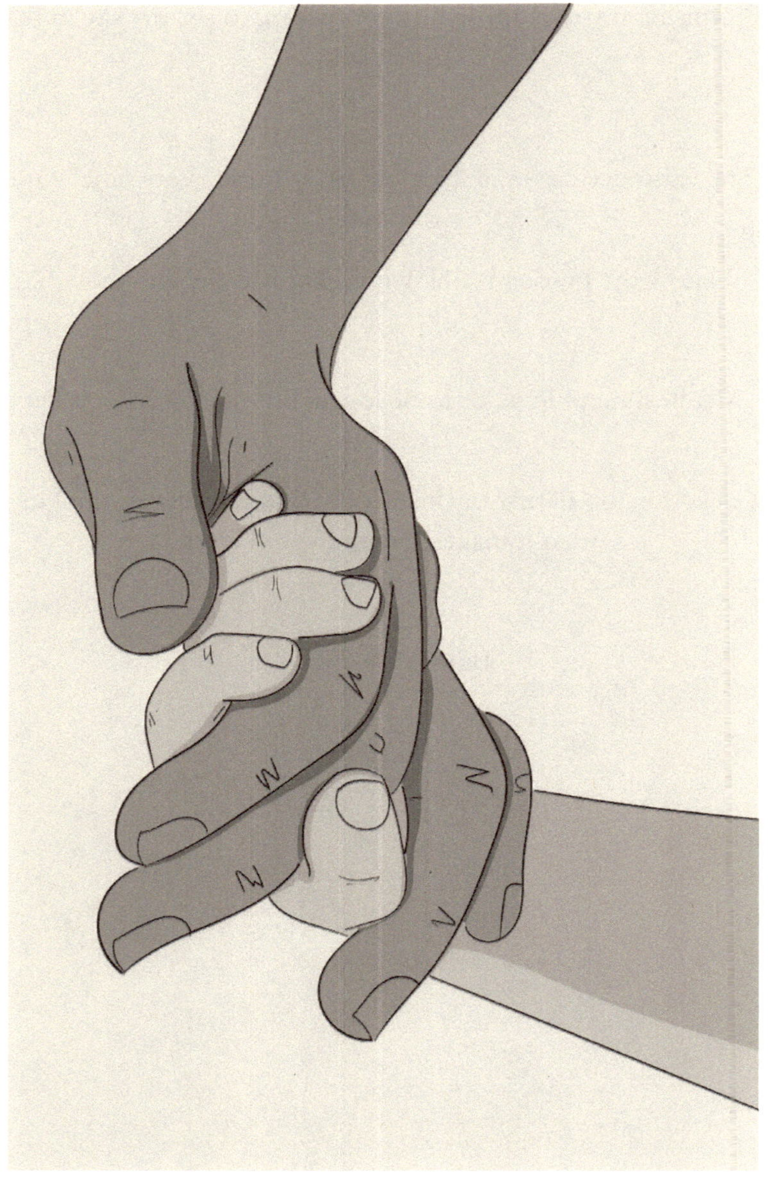

For the souls who are departed and left
to fight with Hippocrates,
since this wasn't the part of childhood puzzle game.

You got heaven gives Peace to me,
just like the way my smile gave it to you,
My heart felt every day,

couldn't decide how to balance and
filter the tear of pain and fear

My fragmented soul wailed under every lamp,
and corner of my dwell in this earthly hell

U dusted me with values of gold and it's
further debt, but still it wasn't the part of childhood bet

Shipping and sailing in emotional tranquillity to
get more peace and love that you gave,
I wish I could refund it once again.
I wish I could meet my dad again.

8

A dream

Can I be verbose today?

Since that's the only freedom I am left with

I sometimes doubt, whether Are philosophers less understood or whether humans sometimes doubt their existence;

Was caged and shut down for I shouted and expressed, and that became the only value I own when I recognized myself according to the syllabi of society;

building my museums in dark hazy mountains, don't want to be kissed by ghosts anymore, walking two more steps ahead when I get Doubtful about my worth socially and biologically when I don't remain a poet anymore but a rebel who curses patriarchy,

Am I really sovereign or just blended and splendid like mere Hippocrates with the worst protocols this society demands me!

One day will grace out my sword to kill oneself, maybe the only tactic I am left with;

Filtered splashes of the sun when kissed my swollen face with love and whispered, "god loves you, and you exist for a purpose to be someone else's blessing ", their reality came as a cynical and threatened dream,

Touching the skies where I don't feel decayed, wish to recite my songs in a place where I fall in love every time with the nectar of being liberal. Don't know how to live, but being brave enough to live, at least with everything that fuels life in me.

9

This middle age defines what?

Exploited childhood? Or the books which were like stars
those days, whispering from distance not to lose hope

to This feeble upcoming old age

Whose veins and arteries are made out of love and need
warmth in return.

Which manuscript says a woman is a

Piece of decorative sex?

Who desperately needs heart-aching ointment during freaking
calling old-age.

But I still cry at every dominant, usual slap that makes my
cheeks unnaturally red with imprinted fingers, leaving me
solely lifeless.

Liveried in a costume of age, where wearing hypocrisy is
digestible, but types of denim are still questionable on my
skin,

None waits for me, except those unclean utensils kept on
shiny marbles that know my struggles for years.

This middle age defines what?

I miss my Crescent shape brows, but I am frequently being
ignored by my mirror for avoiding facial scars and unwanted
pregnancies during the age of menopause

That is still killing new-born daughters,

Yes, I secretly tell my stories to my soaring and restless pillows well-coordinated with my heartbeats and clock tik - tik during early dawns,

I have my coordinated affairs with my tea at irregular early AM's that validates my hopes sometimes,

From fabrics of reds now to deep browns that shows my hazy wrinkles, grey hair cordially defining my headaches I took to get spaces between my own types of blood,

Here I write a letter to myself!

My 'Me' time visits for 'kajras' are replaced by outings that are no more mine or mine. Stuck like a web on walls don't know, this mid-age defines what?

10

Beauty that wasn't meant to fade

Mirror on the grey wall doesn't
pleases my wrinkles in sixties,

Neither I am jealous of one's
whose beauty doesn't fade ever;

Dark hazy bushes and the restless
porcupine freezing at winter seven
that are just a piece of sombre
For my wreaked knees,

My cheeks still flush with pleasure with faded
crumbled old dresses on unknown young calls,

Seems as if ice like eyes have again
kept on my heart for trial again;

It wasn't a strange perfume, I was guessing
long back on rail compartments in my stalking
and candy licking years
with a man like Arabian steed four steps away,

The age when I risked every thug for a mad passion;
Can sympathize for every blot but not suffering,

some caring echoes still
haunt me not to visit dark and absurd
moors with hounds roaring from aesthetic orchards,

It is not about the injured stitches of
infatuation that killed inner realm
but also, that motherhood
that never came with baby cries;

Yellow daffodils on park street -11
still calls shivering hands,
Broken initiatives and
Pleasing lips to wear fragrances;

Will never curse those lilac candles
for lighting my jittery years,
But hideous faithless time
When I didn't trust my soul

that remained dead while

fuelling myself to experience more truth,

sharing my energies to mannequins

to acknowledge my brave rides,

while shaking the dust from my wings tonight.

11

Unite the broken threads of my fairy world

Connected like unbroken whorls that have defines
flinching of hearts that wails for the world with
no parasite of hate and jealousy.

When freedom of huge orchards reveals the
elation of women in dark bushes of Burkina Faso
will not be mutilated, and their pleasures will gain dignity;

Hunters won't be criminals for tusks and skin and
faunas will deserve free air and not be trivial any more,

When we are not a hubris towards each other,
with our long fingers that will not be fumbling
and numb before thoughtless imbecile;

Waiting for that even air of solitude that digests
the pains of surrogacy and the ones who dump their 'new-born',

When eyelashes won't be wet,
wailing for their soul husbands who are now a martyr,
and apologies will no more be an

act of manipulation to reach benefits;

That will be moment of opulence when

toddlers of Syria and Uighurs ones seek

music wearing colours of love and hears

music that rolls peace rather of bombardment,

the time when their fathers won't justify by that it's a family game,

That telescope when gives me the serenity

of wandering places where men will not be a fickle womanizer,

flourishing places with both saffron and green when humanity balances monotheism and polytheism, and I long for them too;

Will admire walking on streets that hold them

eyes respectfully for whores, and to the lands where prairies of lovers will be blessed with no warnings to kill,

let me jump onto the bandwagon when

sapiens don't switch loyalties,

To lure the time when pianos won't wail

long and lyrics won't put that

corner girl into broken nostalgia;

Will my 'will' boat sail on the same ocean?
When fragile libs and thin thighs won't swallow their saliva
and bleed for food and thirst,
where the temple-like globe I believe in.

12

Do you have any?

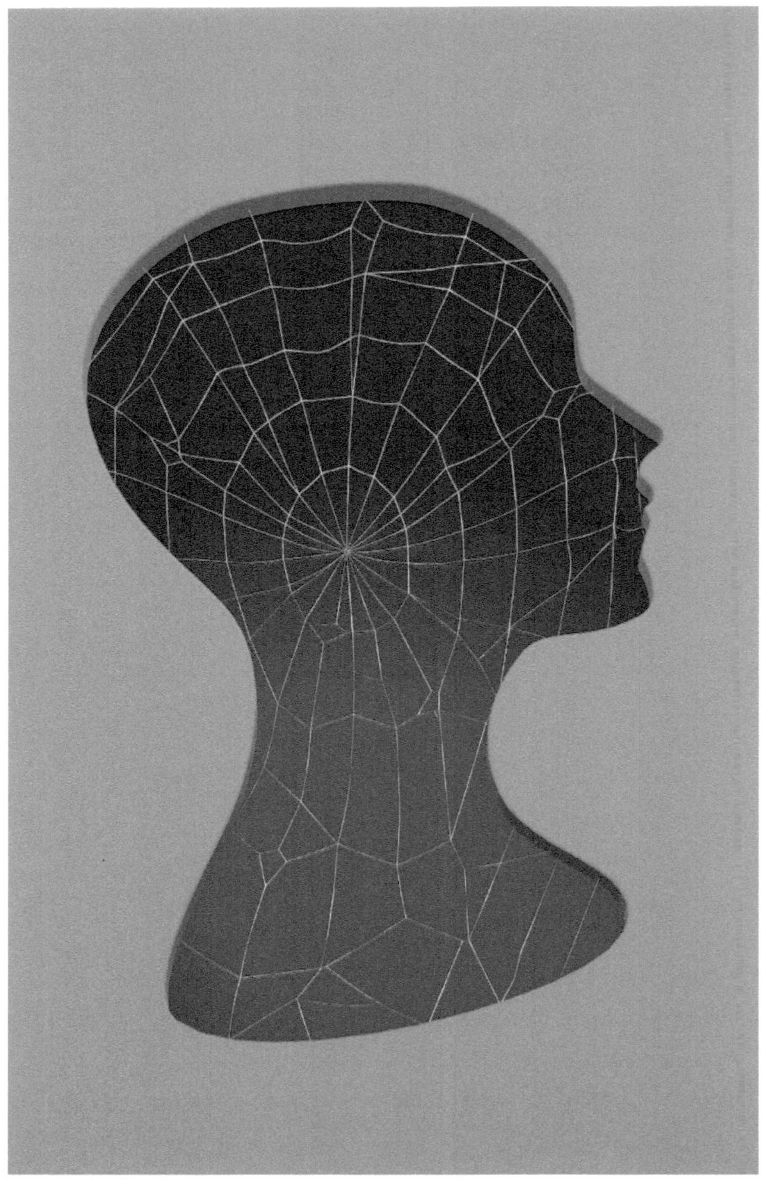

Do you have one?

Asking that giant banyan tree,

Do You have someone to lean on?

Who is gazing at me like an absurd?

While I was a 'lavender moor girl' watching his girls' videos

was his dream as he lost hope to find her again.

Remembering year's back-littered Saturdays

When emotions were just a click away

that follows till dawn,

arguing with the pup outside,

Do you have someone to cry on?

Wiggling his talent with dirt to express

Zillions of licks.

Fathoms of ruptures eagerly waiting in a queue to question!

I think it wishes to make me cry at odd times of the day,

Mocking!

"You alone?"

And like a blunt sorrowful, disdainful,

Grumpy woman questioning my loneliness,

asking that banyan tree

With its figs.

I will be in the Parisian travelling museums of Zurich in my dream

Do you have an Eiffel to mesmerize with?

Do you have someone to lean on?

13

Alpha Me

Have known the threshold of temples,

Endlessly jiggling of bells not judging my metaphysical being

I am in silence,

Sadly wrapping my cautions with slow

Chats and trembling hands,

Air has a solace counting my steps

Towards Jupiter, Saturn and Mars.

Being the goddess of my 'Alpha story'

And being 'Alpha women's

When banalities pondered,

When roses in my orchards didn't love me,

Ring finger lost its faith.

Ok! I will gulp everything on Sunday afternoon,

On welcoming pillows

and also murmur

In the streets of Auckland with

street fellows,

surrendering my guts to

the mountain during

Lazy winters that haven't

shown light since last winter.

Have distributed my rages on leftover

Dusty diaries and

Also decorated with never-ending ink

Of wisdom, pain, and jealousy sipped coffees.

I am calm,

Solemn,

At peace, consolidating my

Semantic self.

14

For the ones who are sorry

What do you think crusades were?

A religious tug?

Maybe a ruthless, and act of dumbness that caused a massive massacre,

Or I should say you wore emeralds and batches of major egoism.

Like you walked miles to reach holy land on the carpets of your own bloodshed

And then shamelessly

asking your god to acquire extended lands,

From where did you your pupils got enough courage to kill little toddlers, and already helpless women that you were always insecure about, peacefully sleeping souls who didn't relish next day Ramadan,

I'm sorry you have caused enough filth in your own shrines,

beautified with cursed cries and sprinkled with murdered blood;

You hold crown of hypocrisy

A tongue that is fraud,

A soul that is dishonest,

And your skin that changes after every prayer,

Your deeds never correspond with scriptures you flaunt

any expect your almighty to shower grace's upon you,

And also expecting this pandemic to end, when somewhere you had and have sold your souls for few pennies,

Always craving for horsepower and money

hoping it doesn't come out of your pockets when you die off...

15

Not every time

It's not every time I am spelling something,

Not every hour I wait;

May be not a grudge that I am holding

which is making me more vulnerable

to attend innocent faces.

I am absolute, that last line of poetry

Who doesn't wish to get over.

I am more of a "coma" laden soul that meets

Nightingales;

I frequently visit my old diaries

with a lamp with me,

It reminds me of Siliguri tales

Addressing my tresses that belong to the

Mountains and the warmth of winters.

I walk as Pre assumed dream that ends with many eclipses for some dark bushes.

I try!

I always try to run away with a goal while keeping,

glances over those eyes giving tap-tap on my shoulders.

Sometimes seeking 'gods' silhouette in the sky above

This is why I say, it's not every time I am spelling something.

Settling myself in madness, Subtle but with a lack of patience

because it's not every time I observe

'Not every time' I wait!

16

At the door

There is a strength that I hold
not to breathe that air at the door, the count up to one, two, three.
To judge its synchronization with my fourth beat,

It splashes my face with hope for some days
but on that ninth Sunday
It splashes itself to be too insecure and Blake

I asked those formal breezes for the conspiracy they hold with my bedsheets,
Somehow they struggle to surface me and left it on the road as clueless and unresolved,

Several faces of air wait at exit doors, alluring my subconscious, but I think the way consolidate myself with last sip of coffee that shuts all the gloomy air that claims to be too hypothetical.

17

It's been a while

It's been a while

Haven't questioned my boiling,

An interrupted air often greets me at every window;

Splashes of abuses

Knock my pupil,

Sun knows my colours,

Moon knows my virtues,

bringing stars to love me again.

My regrets consolidate me at that

hour,

when my Mondays show me it's face

And Sunday leaves an illusion of dramatic comfort;

Haven't picked this stress at three dawns,

It evolves,

It generates,

It calms,

but it comes again,

It comes again!

18

I could do

I have been swallowing the rushes

Of old souls who have come back to give enlightenment and new hopes with crushing possibilities for crystal me.

The revolution hasn't been over yet,

the time hasn't put me down yet.

It revolves

It comes back

Eating the innermost nerve of my brain

I am not searching for anxiety.

It searches for me.

Why I am even wandering with the ones who

never believed my raptures?

Who never believed the quality of sleep I deserve?

Why consent is not so true for some.

Not believing myself, is doubting!

That's the proudest thing I could not do.

No regrets yet!

19

All I know is beautiful

I don't know anything about being fragile
All I know is that beauty is always been
an overrated weight
And an underrated punishment

People think and focus on things of beauty belong
In museums so every time someone calls
My smile, my hair, my feet, my hands,
My body, my lips, my eyes, my liners as
'beautiful'
I build myself a museum to Store all the moments
That I have been overrated
Because beauty is like the war,
People just know it was waged,
But they don't know
They are the mammoth left behind, tasting it's

Disgracefulness by-products.

So let me enlighten you in my
own ugly way, about what beauty is,
About what it means to be
The baby embryo growing in a test tube
In a World of increasing birth rates
About what it means to have no idea
About your body but still be used as a bookmark
About it means to be an adjective
And not a noun.

I don't know anything about being fragile
Maybe it's useless to be made of glass
In a crowd of plastic and wood,

But then it's easier to find yourself when lost;
Just listen to the clinks,
The cracks, and the excessive light that you involuntarily reflect,

I don't know anything about being fragile
But sunset preach
Eyelashes propose,
Hiccups grieve, and missed calls stay longer in our hearts
Than the last time someone calls as 'beautiful'

(Because fragility is never accepted as art, so I now carry a note on me that says "handle with care ")

20

How much to hold?

I am actually not talking about flares of
Orange sky,
But that childhood which was not nourished
I am not talking about the time I spare on swiping left;
to wait for something to happen for seconds to blush me;
But maybe that numbness due to betrayals
The ones who are carrying rented hearts with coloured
waters;
It's been time,
A hell time!
When a conclusion is hard to get.
Right now trust is like a tongue
That hasn't got the script of loyalty,
How much to hold?
How much to wait for the dawn to meet dusk?
Will shut all the Programmable views
from rigid houses and minds,
And configure for peace that will always be
my kind.

21

My Initiatives with me

A Thousand times you Burry me

to shape my worthlessness,

I am certainly not the descendant of meekness,

Call me the cactus of 'Arabian Land' instead!

Can you light up my deserted initiatives??

I have been swallowing them bit by bit

since my innocence,

I will be much happier when

I stop earning my smile,

When an always "yes" Becomes an absolute "no",

I have been struggling with different 'oceans'

calling me to join their 'sorrow eve',

I have already left all my smiles way back glancing at 'balloon sky',

Brick by brick I start building myself in the morning,

but somehow evening teases me with decades of grudges.

I have a swollen fate that needs nourishment

to feast myself with the turkey of peace

and love under bridges,

give me tangerine of love that I had spelled

In vineyards alone.

22

Graded anxiety

My thoughts keep me alive

They come in a sequence of pleasure

And slow down with hope disguised

With swollen aches;

I keep falling in love with dreams that

take me towards coffee dates with my lipstick beautifying those mugs,

Then I murmur gossip with those smudged liners for being betrayed;

My nerves are tired asking me if I was asking too much in return,

I don't want love to be a common failure.

Minutes pass with graded anxiety,

Tick-tick - tick- tick still questions

If I am still awake or live??

My tears know the distance that goes from

Eye till chin

giving condolences to my chapped lips

That no longer entertain virtual dates

Let my subconscious decide if I need to sleep

And cuddle my patience

Flowing with the flow.

23

What I have left

What I have left with

give me a sound of half regret

disguised with half condolences,

it seems like an old cloth

That has lost its color but

still takes the charge

To prepare its purpose.

There is a nerve that takes responsibility to digest

Blame, falling for the ring finger mostly

That finger faces faithlessness after every snow

And then wipes its eyes with no guilt till

every summer!

My poetry has a deep rhythm that

makes the sound of

Dhap! Dhap! Dhap!

It makes its way from every quarter till new year self-care eve, sheltered with

the darkest hours.

Series of lifetime suspense,

still continuous till dusky

sky.

Are you trying to ask that poet to die in the mid of the night
for an hour,

and then revive for people with morning jerks,

that dawn keeps me in a dilemma

of peace and chaos;

words of my poetry do not bend

for people,

since I haven't taught my virtues to take filth.

In those daisies, hazy hours I lay quiet!

Monotonous but full of love.

24

Come Back

I have been changing rainbows in mid of that rainy day,
sometimes it remains an illusion of banality,

But I was deeply scared.

His corner eyelashes stuck with me for hours,

Wish to grope your soul during a full moon.

I belong to that Arabian land where I have served you wine in walnut glasses,

that have shadowed dryness now.

I have been taken away by the silk you wore

Which is much lustrous like our need

to see each other after every confirmed delay,

My anxiety reaches every graded level

when eye contacts remain weak as

Our frozen trust,

I promise I will put lengths of hugs after

Every argument with a complementary tight pinch,

Not to become arid in dry spaces because we deserve daffodils,

Let rainfall embrace us before rainbow pretends and show its shaded in uneven weather.

Like a silly jumping girl who wants to sing a rhyme of vowels
with you at that pitch where our intimacy meets,

Where hearts meet for eye's to roar,

And pupils stuck for lips to have a never-ending glare,

I have seen all 28 moons in you.

Let's not move the mountains of ecstasy

Eyes are dissolving,

they see you mysteriously,

They wait.

Come back!

25

There is a girl

There is a girl that I scream for
Night and day I heal for
She is a live sonnet I keep reading on
Finding that virtue to bring it on

I keep asking those skies to get her on the bridge
And skies yell every time with no glitch,

There is a girl that I scream for
Night and day I heal for
She is a live sonnet I keep reading on
Finding that virtue to bring it on

There is a romance I set at twelve
In your eyes to dwell
I have been loving slow motion clips
Behind the curtains where our heart sniffs

There is a faith I collide with
A fear of losing you,
Hug me until its Sunday

Till reaching bloody Monday,

There is a girl that I scream for

Night and day, I heal for.

26

Before I was a poet, everything has its place

Before I was a poet, everything has its place

To be the part of even the full stops,

snuggling till the time I get perfect sleep;

League of thoughts running behind every end of eyelashes

My nails have bathed itself to the wine of flexes on nautical beds,

with spacious league between my collar bones,

and they are auspiciously being so dramatic to give a thought about how I felt after sunset,

Sunsets are exciting;

But too melodramatic for monologue actress like me.

Followed by the glare! Glare! And then glares again.

Because before I was a poet, everything has its place.

Because centuries of thoughts away I have been in a legit relationship with some raw numbness, practice to cure it step by step, counting the faithful skies that don't warm me to leave on weekends,

Because Before I was a poet, everything has its place

But they were the definite blankets that I carry to escape from monotonous walls Who didn't allow me to watch sunsets, when people became unknown to me to give birthday wishes to fulfil formal burden,

Doubting, criticizing, like a cute Cadbury girl on human generic on Saturdays so that it gets compensated with my midnight sweets.

Because Before I was a poet, everything has its place.

(the world is so unknown about the efforts that we put in and consider it as bleak with generosity offered to them but no it is a life where we are, and we will be taught and redeemed for).

www.ingramcontent.com/pod-product-compliance
Lightning Source LLC
LaVergne TN
LVHW090043160826
845672LV00013B/629
* 9 7 8 9 3 9 0 5 6 7 4 5 4 *